LEGENDS IN THE MAKING

BASKETBALL LEGENDS IN THE MAKING

BY MATT DOEDEN

CAPSTONE PRESS
a capstone imprint

Sports Illustrated Kids Legends in the Making are published by Capstone Press, 1710 Roe Crest Drive, North Mankato, Minnesota 56003
www.capstonepub.com

Library of Congress Cataloging-in-Publication Data
Doeden, Matt.
  Basketball legends in the making / by Matt Doeden.
      pages cm.—(Sports illustrated kids. Legends in the making)
  Includes index.
  ISBN 978-1-4765-4063-4 (library binding)
  ISBN 978-1-4765-5189-0 (paperback)
1. Basketball players—Biography—Juvenile literature. I. Title.
  GV884.A1D62 2014
  796.3230922—dc23   2013032771

Editorial Credits
Anthony Wacholtz, editor; Ted Williams, set designer; Terri Poburka, designer;
     Eric Gohl, media researcher; Jennifer Walker, production specialist

Printed in the United States of America in Stevens Point, Wisconsin.
102014   008565R

TABLE OF CONTENTS

The National Basketball Association has always been loaded with stars, from Wilt Chamberlain to Michael Jordan. Which of today's NBA stars are on their way to greatness? Turn the page to discover some of the league's most talented players.

KEVIN DURANT

POSITION:
SMALL FORWARD

HEIGHT:
6 FEET 9 INCHES
(206 CM)

WEIGHT:
215 POUNDS
(98 KG)

COLLEGE:
UNIVERSITY
OF TEXAS

NBA TEAM:
OKLAHOMA CITY THUNDER

Kevin Durant may be the best scorer in the NBA today. The Oklahoma City Thunder forward is a true playmaker who can create shots and get his team moving. Durant can shoot from the **perimeter**, drive to the basket, or pull up and shoot **mid-range jumpers**. His wide range of skills makes him almost impossible to defend.

The Seattle SuperSonics drafted Durant second overall in 2007. He was an instant star. He averaged 20.3 points per game as a rookie. The team moved to Oklahoma City in 2008, and Durant really started to shine. In his third season, he averaged 30.1 points per game to lead the NBA in 2009–10. He went on to lead the league in scoring the next two seasons as well.

Durant's best season may have been 2011–12. He led the Oklahoma City Thunder to the NBA Finals, but they lost to the Miami Heat. Many experts believe it's only a matter of time before Durant wins a championship of his own.

⇨ Did You Know?

Durant wears number 35 to honor his childhood coach, Charles Craig. His coach died at age 35.

PERIMETER—the area near and beyond the three-point line, far from the basket

MID-RANGE JUMPER—a shot that's inside the three-point line, but not close to the basket

Chris Paul of the Los Angeles Clippers is one of the greatest point guards in the NBA. He uses his quickness to drive to the basket. He has great **court vision** and can sneak passes to open teammates. Paul is even better on defense. His quick hands have put him on the top of the league for steals.

The New Orleans Hornets drafted Paul in 2005. His 175 steals as a **rookie** were the most in the NBA. Paul also averaged 16.1 points and 7.8 assists—stats that earned him Rookie of the Year honors. He went on to lead the league in total steals in five of his first seven seasons. He even set a record by getting at least one steal in 108 straight games.

The Hornets traded Paul to the Clippers in 2011. The Clippers quickly became one of the league's top teams. Paul has also enjoyed success with Team USA, winning Olympic gold medals in 2008 and 2012.

⤷ Did You Know?

Paul is also an excellent bowler. He is part owner of a pro bowling team.

COURT VISION—the ability to see what all the players on the court are doing and understand how a play will unfold

ROOKIE—a first-year player

CHRIS
PAUL

POSITION:

POINT GUARD

HEIGHT:	WEIGHT:
6 FEET (183 CM)	175 POUNDS (79 KG)

COLLEGE:
WAKE FOREST
UNIVERSITY

NBA TEAMS:
NEW ORLEANS HORNETS,
LOS ANGELES CLIPPERS

LaMARCUS ALDRIDGE

POSITION:
POWER FORWARD

HEIGHT:	WEIGHT:
6 FEET 11 INCHES (211 CM)	240 POUNDS (109 KG)

COLLEGE:
UNIVERSITY OF TEXAS

NBA TEAM:
PORTLAND TRAIL BLAZERS

LaMarcus Aldridge of the Portland Trail Blazers may be the best offensive power forward in the NBA. He uses his height and long **wingspan** to dominate down low. But Aldridge can also step back and shoot a jumper from outside. His smooth moves and efficient shot make him tough to defend.

Aldridge was a star at the University of Texas before coming to the NBA in 2006. He steadily improved his rookie season and became a valuable part of the Trail Blazers. Aldridge really began to shine in 2010–11. He averaged 21.8 points and 8.8 rebounds per game. He was named to the All-NBA Third Team. He played in the All-Star Game in 2012 and 2013.

Aldridge is a physical player in the post on both sides of the ball. His offensive skill set makes him one of the most dangerous forwards in the league.

⇨ Did You Know?

Aldridge suffers from a rare heart condition called Wolff–Parkinson–White syndrome. It sometimes causes his heart to beat too quickly. Doctors help Aldridge manage his condition so he can stay on the court.

WINGSPAN—a measure of a player's width, with arms outstretched, from fingertip to fingertip

Forward Carmelo Anthony has been a scoring machine since he entered the league in 2003. "Melo" has averaged more than 20 points per game in every season he's played. Anthony is a threat from inside or outside. He uses his quickness to blow past defenders. Or he steps back and launches long-range shots. His ability to shoot or drive makes him a nightmare for opposing defenders.

Anthony spent one year in college before entering the NBA. He led Syracuse to an NCAA title in 2003 and was named Most Outstanding Player of the NCAA Tournament. He became an instant star with the Denver Nuggets, who selected him third overall in the 2003 NBA Draft. Anthony led the Nuggets to the Western Conference Finals in 2009.

Denver traded Anthony to the New York Knicks in 2011. Anthony led the Knicks to playoff appearances in 2011, 2012, and 2013. He also won the NBA scoring title in 2013, averaging 28.7 points per game.

Did You Know?

Anthony has earned medals on three U.S. Olympic basketball teams. He is the all-time leading scorer for Team USA.

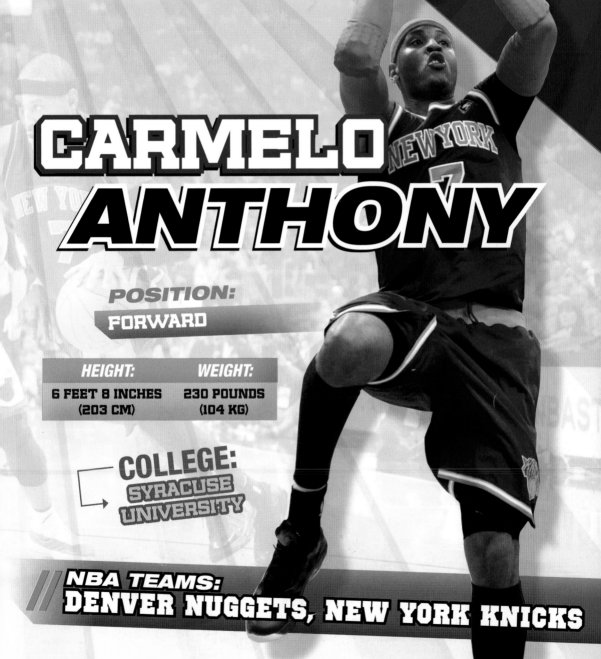

CARMELO ANTHONY

POSITION:
FORWARD

HEIGHT:	WEIGHT:
6 FEET 8 INCHES (203 CM)	230 POUNDS (104 KG)

COLLEGE:
SYRACUSE UNIVERSITY

NBA TEAMS:
DENVER NUGGETS, NEW YORK KNICKS

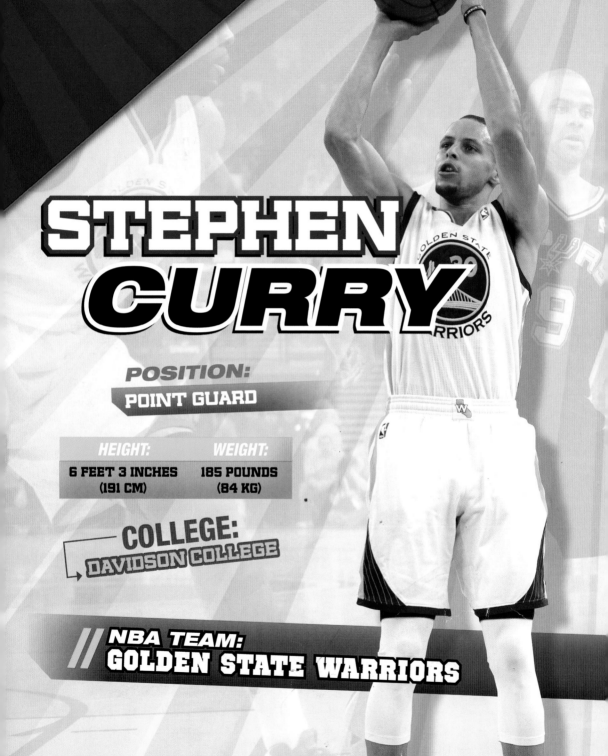

STEPHEN CURRY

POSITION:

POINT GUARD

HEIGHT:	WEIGHT:
6 FEET 3 INCHES (191 CM)	185 POUNDS (84 KG)

COLLEGE:
DAVIDSON COLLEGE

NBA TEAM:
GOLDEN STATE WARRIORS

Stephen Curry is a pure shooter. The Golden State Warriors guard can hit a shot from anywhere on the court. He averages more than two three-pointers per game and is one of the best free throw shooters in the NBA.

Curry has basketball in his blood. His father, Dell, was an NBA player, assistant coach, and TV broadcaster. Dell, like Stephen, was a sharpshooting guard. He helped teach Stephen his nearly flawless jump shot.

In his three years at Davidson College, Curry set the school record for points with 974. But NBA teams wondered if he could play at the professional level. The Warriors believed he could and picked him seventh overall in the 2009 NBA Draft. Curry has since rewarded them by becoming one of the league's most dangerous shooters. In 2013 he knocked down 272 three-pointers, the best single-season total in NBA history.

⤷ Did You Know?

Curry made 162 three-pointers with Davidson in 2007–08, a single-season NCAA record.

Power forward Blake Griffin is a human highlight reel. Los Angeles Clippers fans love to cheer on his high-flying **alley-oops** and thunderous dunks. But Griffin can do a lot more than just dunk the ball. He's also one of the game's best rebounders, and he can pass the ball well for a power forward.

Griffin played college ball at Oklahoma, where he was national player of the year in 2009. He was the number one pick of the 2009 NBA Draft. Griffin completely missed the next NBA season with an injury. But he came back strong in 2010–11. He averaged 22.5 points per game and was the league's rookie of the year.

Griffin's scoring average has dipped since 2011. But he has worked on his all-around game. He has become a better mid-range shooter, and his defense is greatly improved. With his natural athletic ability, intensity, and work ethic, there's no telling how good he can become.

⤳ Did You Know?

Griffin won the NBA's Slam Dunk Contest in 2011 by jumping over a car and jamming the ball.

ALLEY-OOP—a move in which a player leaps up near the basket to catch a pass and make a basket, usually a dunk

BLAKE GRIFFIN

POSITION:
POWER FORWARD

HEIGHT:	WEIGHT:
6 FEET 10 INCHES (208 CM)	251 POUNDS (114 KG)

COLLEGE:
UNIVERSITY OF OKLAHOMA

NBA TEAM:
LOS ANGELES CLIPPERS

DERRICK ROSE

POSITION:

POINT GUARD

HEIGHT:	WEIGHT:
6 FEET 3 INCHES	190 POUNDS
(191 CM)	(86 KG)

COLLEGE:
UNIVERSITY OF MEMPHIS

NBA TEAM:
CHICAGO BULLS

Derrick Rose is one of the NBA's most dominant guards. He's a great all-around player. He can take it to the basket, shoot from outside, or dish out assists. He's also an excellent defender. There isn't much Rose can't do.

The Chicago Bulls drafted Rose first overall in 2008. Rose was an instant star. He earned Rookie of the Year honors in 2009. The following year, he played in his first All-Star Game. Then in 2011 he averaged 25 points and 7.7 assists per game. He was named the league's **Most Valuable Player**.

Injuries have plagued Rose since his MVP season. He played in just 39 games in 2011–12 and missed all of 2012–13. But Bulls fans hope he'll soon regain his MVP form.

Did You Know?

Derrick Rose was 22 years old when he was named MVP, becoming the youngest player in NBA history to earn the award.

MOST VALUABLE PLAYER (MVP)—an award given to the player who does the most to help his team win

James Harden's smooth moves and ability to attack the basket have made him a scoring threat in the NBA. Harden is a great playmaker with the skills to drive the lane or step back and shoot threes.

Oklahoma City picked Harden third overall in the 2009 NBA Draft. He started out as a bench player. In three years with the Thunder, he started only seven games. But that didn't mean he wasn't a star. He was an important spark in the Thunder lineup and played a huge role in their run to the NBA Finals in 2012. That season Harden averaged 16.8 points off the bench and was named Sixth Man of the Year, an award given to the best non-starting player.

The Thunder traded Harden to the Houston Rockets before the 2012–13 season. Harden instantly became one of the league's leading scorers. He averaged 25.9 points per game and made his first All-Star team.

⤷ Did You Know?

Harden led the Sophomore team with 30 points in the All-Star Rookie Challenge in 2011. The game pits the first-year rookies against the second-year sophomores.

JAMES HARDEN

POSITION:
SHOOTING GUARD

HEIGHT:
6 FEET 5 INCHES
(196 CM)

WEIGHT:
220 POUNDS
(100 KG)

COLLEGE:
ARIZONA STATE
UNIVERSITY

NBA TEAMS:
OKLAHOMA CITY THUNDER,
HOUSTON ROCKETS

RAJON RONDO

POSITION:
POINT GUARD

HEIGHT:	WEIGHT:
6 FEET 1 INCH (185 CM)	171 POUNDS (78 KG)

COLLEGE:
UNIVERSITY OF KENTUCKY

NBA TEAM:
BOSTON CELTICS

Rajon Rondo is a good shooter and can create his own shot, but that's not what makes him great. He is a pass-first point guard. He has amazing court vision and always seems to make the right pass at the right time. Rondo is also a solid defender. He's twice been named to the All-NBA Defensive first team. And he's always among the league leaders in steals.

Rondo played at the University of Kentucky before entering the NBA with the Boston Celtics in 2006. Rondo became Boston's starting point guard in 2007–08. He had a strong regular season and an even better postseason. His clutch play helped the Celtics win an NBA championship.

Fans love to watch Rondo pull off a killer crossover dribble or fire a pass on a fast break. His pass-first approach is a big part of what makes him one of the league's brightest stars.

Did You Know?

Rondo started a charity called the Rajon Rondo Foundation to help kids in need.

"King" James is the most complete player in the NBA today. He can do it all. He's a great scorer, brilliant passer, and tireless defender. James is able to play guard or forward, and he can defend any position on the court. It's no wonder he's a four-time league MVP.

Basketball fans knew James' name while he was still in high school in Akron, Ohio. His strong body and natural skill caught the attention of NBA scouts everywhere. The Cleveland Cavaliers selected him first overall in the 2003 draft. James did not disappoint. He averaged 20.9 points per game as a rookie, and he hasn't stopped scoring since.

In 2010 James signed with the Miami Heat. He led the Heat to back-to-back NBA titles in 2012 and 2013. He was named the NBA Finals MVP both times.

⇨ Did You Know?

James was also a star wide receiver on his high school football team. He was named first-team all-state as a sophomore before quitting football to focus on basketball.

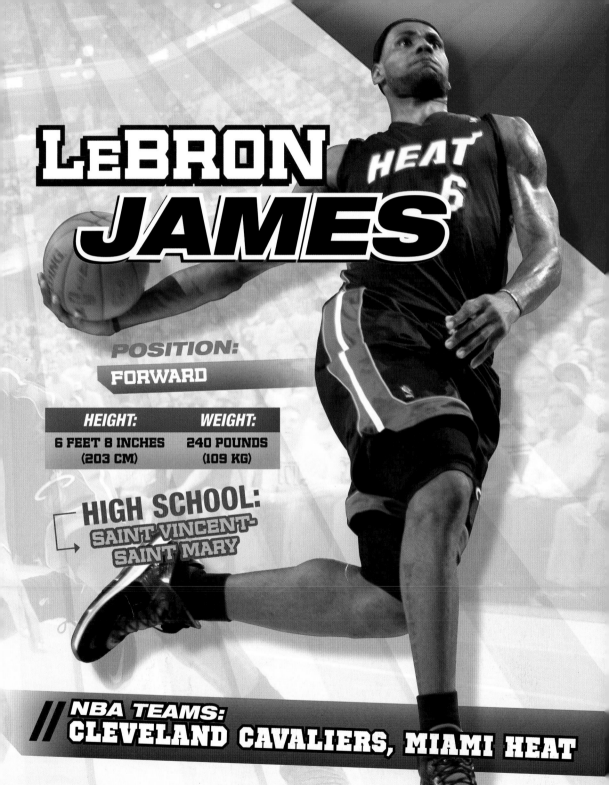

LeBRON JAMES

POSITION:

FORWARD

HEIGHT:	**WEIGHT:**
6 FEET 8 INCHES (203 CM)	240 POUNDS (109 KG)

HIGH SCHOOL:
SAINT VINCENT-SAINT MARY

// **NBA TEAMS:** CLEVELAND CAVALIERS, MIAMI HEAT

KEVIN LOVE

POSITION:
POWER FORWARD

HEIGHT:	WEIGHT:
6 FEET 10 INCHES (208 CM)	260 POUNDS (118 KG)

COLLEGE:

UCLA

NBA TEAM:
MINNESOTA TIMBERWOLVES

Kevin Love is a rebounding machine. He's not the biggest or strongest power forward in the NBA. But his amazing, footwork, hustle, and ability to figure out where the ball will bounce makes him one of the league's top rebounders. Love is also a great pure shooter. He even won the NBA Three-Point Shootout contest in 2012.

Love spent one year at the University of California, Los Angeles (UCLA), before entering the 2008 NBA Draft. The Memphis Grizzlies used the fifth pick on him, but he was immediately traded to the Minnesota Timberwolves. Love came off the bench for most of his first two seasons. He became a full-time starter in 2010–11 and led the NBA in rebounding with 15.2 per game. He was named the league's Most Improved Player.

Love continued to improve in 2011–12. His 26 points per game were fourth best in the league. But Love struggled with injuries throughout 2012–13. Timberwolves fans hope he comes back stronger than ever.

⇨ Did You Know?

In 2010 Love scored 31 points and grabbed 31 rebounds in one game. It was the NBA's first "30-30" game since 1982.

Oklahoma City's Russell Westbrook is one of the game's most dynamic guards. He has a rare combination of athletic ability, basketball skill, and instinct. He's constantly on the attack, driving toward the basket. His aggressiveness forces defenses to collapse, often opening up teammates for shots. Westbrook is a great finisher. If he's not passing, he's shooting a jumper or throwing down a dunk of his own.

Westbrook helped UCLA reach the Final Four in each of his two seasons in college. As an NBA rookie, Westbrook made an instant impact in 2008–09. He averaged 15.3 points per game and was named to the All-Rookie team. The 2011–12 season was especially memorable. Westbrook averaged 23.6 points and helped the Thunder reach the NBA Finals. Westbrook followed that with another great season in 2012–13. But he got hurt in the playoffs, and the team wasn't the same without him.

⤳ Did You Know?

Westbrook is left-handed, but he learned to shoot with his right hand. He uses his right hand to shoot today.

RUSSELL
WESTBROOK

POSITION:

POINT GUARD

HEIGHT:	WEIGHT:
6 FEET 3 INCHES (191 CM)	187 POUNDS (85 KG)

COLLEGE:

UCLA

NBA TEAM:

OKLAHOMA CITY THUNDER

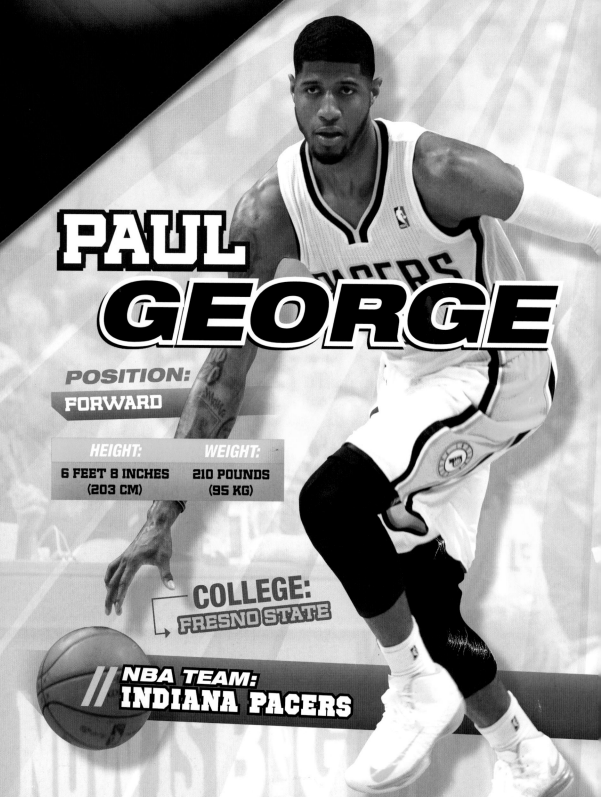

PAUL GEORGE

POSITION:
FORWARD

HEIGHT:
6 FEET 8 INCHES
(203 CM)

WEIGHT:
210 POUNDS
(95 KG)

COLLEGE:
FRESNO STATE

NBA TEAM:
INDIANA PACERS

Forward Paul George can do it all. He can score from inside and out. He's an outstanding rebounder and passer. And he's one of the best defensive players in the NBA. Add it up and you have one of the most complete players in the league.

George has improved every season he's been in the NBA. As a rookie in 2010–11, he averaged just 7.8 points. The next year he increased his scoring to 12.1 points per game. And in 2012–13 he stepped up as Indiana's best player. He scored 17.4 points per game and made the Eastern Conference All-Star Team. He was named the NBA's Most Improved Player.

In the 2013 playoffs, George truly became a star. He stuffed the stat sheet with 19.2 points, 7.4 rebounds, and 5.1 assists per game in the playoffs. He led the surprising Pacers all the way to Game 7 of the Eastern Conference Finals.

⤷ Did You Know?

George recorded a rare triple-double in his first playoff game of 2013. He had 23 points, 12 assists, and 11 rebounds.

RISING STARS

ANTHONY DAVIS

Davis led the Kentucky Wildcats to an NCAA title in 2012. He helped the U.S. men's basketball team to a gold medal at the 2012 Olympics. The number one pick of the 2012 draft thrilled New Orleans fans with his dunks and great defense during his rookie year.

KENNETH FARIED

The Denver Nuggets power forward is nicknamed "Manimal." He is strong and athletic, and he can score, rebound, and block shots.

DAMIAN LILLARD

The Portland Trailblazers guard lit up the NBA as a rookie in 2012–13. His smooth stroke helped him average 19 points per game and win Rookie of the Year honors.

JRUE HOLIDAY

The point guard is a force at both ends of the court. Holiday averaged 14 points and 6.5 assists in his second year with the Philadelphia 76ers. After the 2012–13 season, Holiday was traded to the New Orleans Pelicans.

KEMBA WALKER

The Charlotte Bobcats' guard is an explosive scorer. Walker excels at driving the ball, then dishing to an open teammate.

KYRIE IRVING

The Cavaliers point guard was the league's Rookie of the Year in 2012. Irving is a dynamic playmaker and scorer.

READ MORE

Doeden, Matt. *The Greatest Basketball Records.* Sports Illustrated Kids. Mankato, Minn.: Capstone Press, 2009.

LeBoutillier, Nate. *The Best of Everything Basketball Book.* Sports Illustrated Kids. Mankato, Minn.: Capstone Press, 2011.

Linde, Barbara M. *LeBron James.* New York: Gareth Stevens, 2011.

INTERNET SITES

FactHound offers a safe, fun way to find Internet sites related to this book. All of the sites on FactHound have been researched by our staff.

Here's all you do:

Visit *www.facthound.com*

Type in this code: 9781476540634

Super-cool stuff! Check out projects, games and lots more at **www.capstonekids.com**

INDEX